THE PAJAMA ZOO PARADE

THE FUNNIEST BEDTIME *ABC* BOOK

Author
AGNES GREEN

Illustrated by
ZHANNA MENDEL

It's time for bed... Hip hip hooray! Let's all give a cheer!
The day is through. We've had such fun. Now sleepy time draws near.
So, we'll tidy up our toys and wash our faces clean,
brush our teeth and comb our hair, prepare to rest and dream,

But one important task remains before we say goodnight.
Put on your favorite jammies, and snuggle in real tight.
Before you drift away to dream, let's check in at the zoo.
I hear they're having a parade and a PJ Party too!

A Albert Aloysius will be leading the parade
in neon pink pajamas, and a cap of gold brocade.
He is a proud alpaca, as he marches down the way
while all the others follow, at the end of every day.

Beatrice Baboon is a beauty... all agree,
as she marches through the zoo in her favorite lace nightie.
She smiles at her momma as she marches off to bed,
blowing kisses on her way to rest her pretty head.

Cleopatra, Clyde, and Cooper, still damp from their bath,
follow in their striped pajamas on their scooters down the path.
Papa Cheetah doesn't like it, for he fears they'll catch a chill.
But Cleo, Clyde, and Cooper really don't believe they will.

Desdemona Dingo dances on her toes
in her ballerina nightie, covered all in bows.
Gliding oh so gracefully, she twirls and leaps along.
As she waltzes off to dreamland, she hums her favorite song.

Edward Austin Elephant is cute as he can be.
In his polkadot pajamas, he is quite a sight to see.
He can barely stay awake to the end of the parade,
so he rides in his red wagon pulled along by cousin Wade.

F Fatima Popadopolus is next to come along.
She holds hands with her big brother while they sing a song.
Poppa Popadopolus is proud as he can be.
He is sure his ferret babies will be starring on TV.

Gabrielle Gorilla, with her jammies all in gold,
will not listen to her momma and rarely does what she is told.
Instead of marching with the others, she swings from tree to tree.
That's why Gabrielle Gorilla is a cheeky monkey!

Hugo Hippopotamus with his brother Hans, together,
play upon their banjos as they march in any weather.
In their matching blue pajamas, they strum and stroll on by.
These banjo playing brothers are very happy guys.

Ivan the Iguana doesn't like to go to bed.
He won't pull on his night shirt. He just stands and shakes his head.
After trying to convince him that it is only right,
Ivan's Mamma gave up trying, he sleeps naked every night!

Here comes JJ Jackal in his PJs all of blue
carrying a banner as he marches through the zoo.
He blows his mama kisses as he makes his way to bed.
Little JJ Jackal is a happy sleepy head.

Kimberly Koala is a snuggle bug, it's true.
When it gets close to bedtime at her home here in the zoo,
she is oh so very sleepy, and try though she might,
in her PJs, eyes are closing, off she drifts... Goodnight!

Luna Llama, Leon Leopard, and Linus Lion cub
sail through the parade on a float just for their club.
Their favorite part of bedtime is playing in the bath,
so they wear their sailor jammies rowing slowly down the path.

M
Mia Moose has red pajamas. They button up the back.
She has a matching bathrobe and a plaid night cap.
They are made of flannel so they keep her very warm,
even in bad weather like a winter snow storm.

N Tiny Nina Napu sleeps the whole day through.
Her daytime is our night time, so she's unsure what to do.
Does she take off her pajamas and get dressed to spend the night
awake, alone, and happy until the morning light?

Oliver the Octopus waves flags with all eight limbs.
As he saunters down the sidewalk everybody looks at him.
His snazzy jazzy jammies are red and blue and plaid.
Oliver the Octopus is very seldom sad.

Polly Panda sleeps in jammies yellow as the sun.
When the parade is over and another day is done,
Polly's Papa tucks her in with her blankie all in green.
Then Mommy kisses her goodnight and wishes her sweet dreams.

Quinton Quail and his friend Pete are next in the procession.
The two of them, they have a plan to teach the cat a lesson.
They take their night caps off their heads, and up the tree they fly
and drop them down upon cat as he goes prowling by.

Rabbit Robert Robinson wants to come along
to take part in the parade tonight, but something had gone wrong!
In his hurrying, it seems, there's something he's forgotten...
In racing to get ready, he forgot his PJ bottom!

S Look out for Sammy Seal and his brothers and his sisters.
They balance balls atop their noses, and never muss their whiskers.
Sam can even juggle seven balls upon his head.
In his PJs, with his siblings, Sammy leads them off to bed.

Terrance Tortoise and his cousin, Tony Turtle have the need
to ride atop a fire engine due to lack of speed.
Their PJs look like fire suits and they were custom-made,
by their aunt Petunia 'specially for the bedtime zoo parade.

Upton J. Fitzgerald is a baby urial sheep,
following the others on his way to go to sleep.
He prances off to dreamland. He is always ready
in his favorite pajamas and his soft and fluffy teddy.

V Vera, Vince, and Victor are as proud as they can be
of their velvet green pajamas. They are quite a sight to see.
Mommy Vulture snaps their picture as the three go marching by.
Now the sun has set and the moon is up. Oh my. The day did fly!

W

Wally Walrus waddles past and his night shirt drags along.
As he makes his way toward the end, he hums a sleepy song.
Little Wally's awfully sleepy, getting closer to his bed.
He cannot wait to lay right down and rest his weary head.

Alexander Xantis is a type of yak, it's true.
He wears his fur pajamas as he marches through the zoo.
When you see Alexander, you know it won't be long
before he plays his little drum... Boom, boom, boom, bong!

Now Yolonda Green, the Yorkshire Pup, has chosen well for sleep:
A flannel, tartan nightie, and slippers lined with fleece.
Her sisters and her brothers have saved a little space
so Yolonda Yorkshire Puppy will have a resting place.

Z

Who is this coming down the path? The last one in the line.
It is sweet Sally Zebra, she truly is Devine!
In shiny glitter PJs with purple butterflies,
She twirls and tosses a baton, away up in the sky!

Now you have seen the zoo parade. We've gone from A to Z,
from Albert the Alpaca to a Zebra named Sally.
And now that all the other animals have marched along to bed,
it's your turn to do the same, so lie down and rest your head.

Close your eyes and drift away to dreamland for a while.
And in the morning you will wake, stretch and yawn and smile.
Then we will have more stories, games, adventures—me and you!
Like our friends, the animals, in the PJ party zoo!

PLEASE...

PLEAZZZ

PLEASE, LEAVE A REVIEW!

I hope you enjoyed this cute little story!

Reviews from awesome customers like you

help others to feel confident

about choosing this book too.

Please take a minute to share your experience!

I will be forever grateful.

Yours, Agnes Green

THANK YOU!

"Animals from A to Z are very much like you,
They play, they eat, they sleep, they dream,
They even pee and poo!"

This is a book that answers important potty time questions!